BOOK of DAYS

Book of Days

....

Photography copyright © 1997 by Virginia Dixon

Text copyright © 1997 by Garborg's Heart 'n Home, Inc.

Design by Thurber Creative

Published by Garborg's Heart 'n Home, Inc.

P.O. Box 20132, Bloomington, MN 55420

Scripture quotations marked NIV are taken from the *HOLY BIBLE,*

NEW INTERNATIONAL VERSION® NIV®. Copyright © 1973, 1978,

1984 by International Bible Society. All rights reserved.

Scripture quotations marked TLB are taken from *The Living Bible,*

© 1971. Used by permission of Tyndale House Publishers, Inc.,

Wheaton, IL 60189. All rights reserved.

Printed in Hong Kong.

January

God specializes in things fresh and firsthand.
His plans for you this year may outshine those of the past....
He's preparing to fill your days with reasons to give Him praise.

JONI EARECKSON TADA

January

1

2

3

4

5

6

7

8

January

9

10

11

12

January

13

14

15

16

When we let freedom ring, when we let it ring from every village and every hamlet, from every state and every city, we will be able to speed up that day when all of God's children... will be able to join hands and sing in the words of the old Negro spiritual, "Free at last! Free at last! Thank God Almighty, we are free at last!"

MARTIN LUTHER KING, JR.

January

17

18

19

20

21

22

23

24

January

25

26

27

January

28

29

30

31

February

Among God's best gifts to us
are the people who love us.

February

The best
and most
beautiful things
in the world
cannot be seen
or even
touched.
They must be
felt with the
heart.

HELEN KELLER

1

2

3

4

5

6

7

8

February

9

10

11

12

February

13

14

15

16

February

May your roots go down deep into the soil of God's marvelous love; and may you be able to feel and understand... how long, how wide, how deep, and how high his love really is.

17

18

19

20

February

21

22

23

24

February

25

A friend
is what the
heart needs
all the
time.

HENRY VAN
DYKE

26

27

28

29

March

The year's at spring and day's at morn...
God's in His heaven —
All's right with the world!

ROBERT BROWNING

March

Hold fast
your dreams!
Within your
heart
Keep one still,
secret spot
Where dreams
may go
And, sheltered
so,
May thrive and
grow.

LOUISE
DRISCOLL

1

2

3

4

5

6

7

8

March

9

10

11

12

March

13

14

15

16

Every day in
a life fills the
whole life with
expectation
and memory.

C. S. LEWIS

March

It's the
little things
that make
up the
richest part
of the
tapestry of
our lives.

17

18

19

20

21

22

23

24

March

25

26

27

28

March

29

30

31

It is God to whom and with whom we travel, and while He is the End of our journey, He is also at every stopping place.

ELISABETH ELLIOT

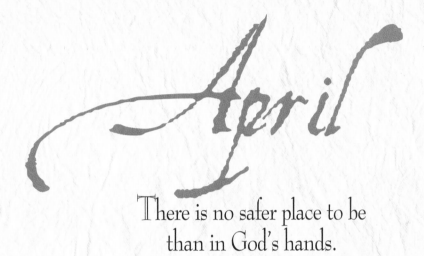

April

There is no safer place to be
than in God's hands.

God loves us; not

but because

He needs to receive

He delights

because we are lovable
He is love, not because
but because

to give.   C. S. LEWIS

April

Jesus cannot forget us; we have been graven on the palms of His hands.

LOIS PICILLO

1

2

3

4

5

6

7

8

April

9

10

11

12

April

13

14

15

16

As Jesus stepped into the garden, you were in His prayers. As Jesus looked into heaven, you were in His vision.... His final prayer was about you. His final pain was for you. His final passion was you.

MAX LUCADO

April

Let the
beloved of the
Lord rest
secure in him,
for he shields
him all day
long, and the
one the Lord
loves rests
between his
shoulders.

DEUTERONOMY
33:12 NIV

17

18

19

20

21

22

23

24

April

25

26

April

27

28

29

30

May

Now may the warming love of friends
surround you as you go
Down the path of light and laughter
where the happy memories grow.

HELEN LOWRIE MARSHALL

May

The joyful
birds prolong
the strain,
their song with
every spring
renewed;
the air we
breathe, and
falling rain,
each softly
whispers:
God is good.

JOHN HAMPDEN
GURNEY

1

2

3

4

May

5

6

7

8

May

9

10

11

12

13

Where your
pleasure is,
there is your
treasure; where
your treasure,
there your
heart; where
your heart,
there your
happiness.

AUGUSTINE

14

15

16

May

For, lo, the winter is past, the rain is over and gone; the flowers appear on the earth; the time of the singing of birds is come.

SONG OF SOLOMON 2:11,12 KJV

17

18

19

20

21

22

23

24

May

25

26

27

28

May

29

30

31

The God who created, names, and numbers the stars in the heavens also numbers the hairs of my head... He pays attention to very big things and to very small ones. What matters to me matters to Him, and that changes my life.

ELISABETH ELLIOT

June

God's bright sunshine overhead,
God's flowers beside your feet...
And by such pleasant pathways led,
May all your life be sweet.

HELEN WAITHMAN

June

Every moment is full of wonder and God is always present.

1

2

3

4

5

6

7

8

June

9

10

11

12

13

14

15

16

We have
been in God's
thought from
all eternity,
and in His
creative love,
His attention
never
leaves us.

❧

MICHAEL
QUOIST

June

May you wake each day with God's blessings and sleep each night in His keeping, and may you always walk in His tender care.

17

18

19

20

21

22

23

24

June

25

26

27

28

29

30

This is the
day the Lord
has made.
We will
rejoice and
be glad in it.

PSALM 118:24
TLB

July

How precious it is, Lord,
to realize that you are thinking about me constantly!
I can't even count how many times a day
your thoughts turn towards me.

PSALM 139:17 TLB

July

Summer
afternoon—
summer
afternoon; to
me those have
always been the
two most
beautiful words
in the English
language.

HENRY JAMES

1

2

3

4

5

6

7

8

July

9

10

11

12

13

14

15

16

Our Creator
would never
have made
such lovely
days, and given
us the deep
hearts to enjoy
them, above
and beyond all
thought, unless
we were meant
to be immortal.

NATHANIEL
HAWTHORNE

July

Today a
new sun
rises for me;
everything
lives,
everything is
animated,
everything
seems to speak
to me of my
passion,
everything
invites me to
cherish it.

ANNE DE
LENCLOS

17

18

19

20

21

22

23

24

July

25

26

27

July

28

29

30

31

Lovely,
complicated
wrappings
Sheath the
gift of
one-day-more;
Breathless, I
untie the
package—
Never lived this
day before!

GLORIA
GAITHER

August

The happiness of life is made up of little things—
a smile, a hug, a moment
of shared laughter.

August

Never lose an opportunity of seeing anything that is beautiful; for beauty is God's handwriting.... Welcome it in every fair face, in every fair sky, in every fair flower, and thank God for it.

RALPH WALDO
EMERSON

1

2

3

4

5

6

7

8

August

9

10

11

12

August

13

14

15

16

God loves
and cares for
us, even to the
least event and
smallest need
of life.

HENRY EDWARD
MANNING

August

May the
Lord bless and
protect you;
may the Lord's
face radiate
with joy
because of you;
may he be
gracious to
you, show you
his favor, and
give you his
peace.

NUMBERS
6:24-26 TLB

17

18

19

20

21

22

23

24

August

25

26

27

28

August

29

30

31

Yesterday is already a dream and tomorrow is only a vision. But today well lived makes every yesterday a dream of happiness and every tomorrow a vision of hope.

Our lives are filled
and blessings
and one of the greatest

with simple joys
without end,
joys in life
is to have a friend.

September

True worth is in *being*, not *seeming*—
In doing, each day that goes by,
Some little good—not in dreaming
Of great things to do by and by.

ALICE CARY

September

1

2

3

4

5

6

7

8

September

9

10

11

12

September

13

14

15

16

Isn't it splendid to think of all the things there are to find out about? It just makes me feel glad to be alive—it's such an interesting world. It wouldn't be half so interesting if we knew all about everything.

LUCY MAUD
MONTGOMERY

September

17

18

19

20

21

22

23

24

September

25

26

27

28

September

29

30

I still find
each day too
short for all the
thoughts I
want to think,
all the walks
I want to take,
all the books
I want to read,
and all the
friends I want
to see. The
longer I live,
the more my
mind dwells
upon the
beauty and
the wonder of
the world.

JOHN
BURROUGHS

October

Love is a fruit in season at all times,
and within the reach of every hand.

MOTHER TERESA

October

God loves
each one
of us as if
there were
only one
of us.

— AUGUSTINE

1

2

3

4

5

6

7

8

October

9

10

11

12

13

14

15

16

Joys come from simple and natural things: mists over meadows, sunlight on leaves, the path of the moon over-water.

SIGURD F. OLSON.

October

17

18

19

20

21

22

23

24

October

25

26

27

28

29

30

31

Trust in the
Lord with all
your heart and
lean not on
your own
understanding;
in all your ways
acknowledge
him, and he
will make your
paths straight.

PROVERBS
3:5,6 NIV

November

Thanks are the highest form of thought,
and gratitude is happiness doubled by wonder.

G. K. CHESTERTON

November

Always new.
Always
exciting.
Always full
of promise.
The mornings
of our lives,
each a personal
daily miracle.

GLORIA
GAITHER

1

2

3

4

5

6

7

8

November

9

10

11

12

November

13

14

15

16

The
goodness of
God is
infinitely
more
wonderful
than we
will ever be
able to
comprehend.

A. W. TOZER

November

17

18

19

20

21

22

23

24

November

25

26

27

28

November

29

30

To be grateful
is to recognize
the love of
God in
everything He
has given us—
and He has
given us
everything.

THOMAS MERTON

December

What can I give Him poor as I am?
If I were a shepherd, I would bring a lamb,
If I were a Wise Man, I would do my part,—
Yet what I can I give Him, give my heart.

CHRISTINA ROSSETTI

December

1

2

3

4

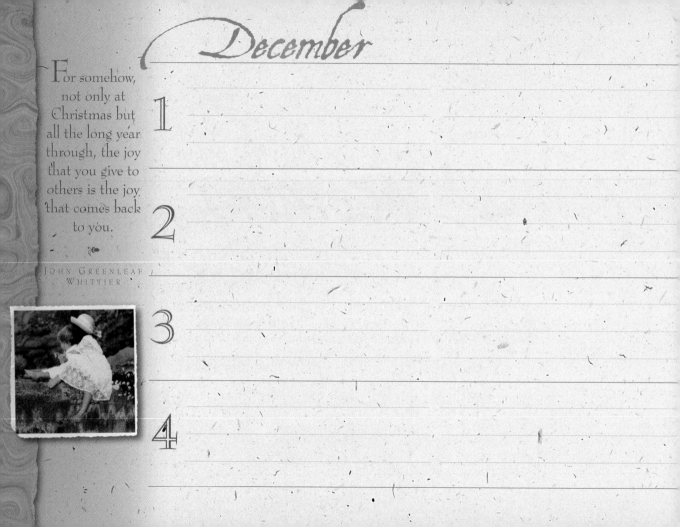

5

6

7

8

December

9

10

11

12

December

13

14

15

16

God grant
you the light
in Christmas,
which is faith,
the warmth of
Christmas,
which is
love...the all
of Christmas,
which is
Christ.

WILDA ENGLISH

December

For to us a child is born, to us a son is given.... And he will be called Wonderful Counselor, Mighty God, Everlasting Father, Prince of Peace.

ISAIAH 9:6 NIV

17

18

19

20

December

21

22

23

24

December

25

26

27

28

December

29

30

31

If we
celebrate
the years
behind us
they become
stepping
stones of
strength
and joy for
the years
ahead.